Riding with the Fireworks

Riding with the Fireworks!

ANN DARR

Library of Congress Catalogue card number 80-70830
ISBN 0-914086-33-2
Printed in the United States of America

Cover design by Amanda Freymann
Cover photo by George deVincent
Typeset by Jeffrey Schwartz
Pasteup by Ed Hogan/Aspect Composition

I want to thank the editors of the following magazines where some
of these poems have appeared: *The Agni Review, Bits, Black and
White Lines, Dryad, Western Poetry Review, Willow Springs
Magazine, Window* and *Poetry Now.*

The publication of this book was made possible with support from the
Massachusetts Council on the Arts and Humanities, a state agency whose
funds are recommended by the Governor and appropriated by the
State Legislature. This project was supported in part by grant from
the National Endowment for the Arts in Washington, D.C., a
federal agency.

Alice James Books
138 Mount Auburn Street
Cambridge, Massachusetts 02138

For Robert and Kathleen

and the crew

of *Point Counterpoint II*

CONTENTS

RIDING WITH THE FIREWORKS

down Mississippi Route 61 to catch up
with the American Wind Symphony Barge

We are bouncing along in the blue
van trying to catch the barge
that ran by Greenville at 10 A M
and kept on traveling down
that center channel going like a bat
out of Helena Arkansas. The lower
the river, the faster the channel
flows.

We have just passed
the road to Hushkapena
and I know for a fact
I will never go there.

Lou takes out his
bass trombone
to show me how
a circular valve
differs from a piston,
and tells me how
his steel co-workers
differ from
musicians
who never would have called him
Trombone Lou.

Here at the Yazoo River, at
Vicksburg where the wrecked train cars
are still crumpled on one track,
where the Atlas Tank Co.'s sign says
"EVERYTHING" on its storage shed,
we are stopped by the Illinois Central Gulf
switching its piggy-back cars. At the River Store
the sign says "POSITIVELY NO CHILDREN OR VISITORS
OR ▮▮▮▮ BEYOND THIS POINT." Could the
blackened blank read FIREWORKS underneath?

Under the front seat of the van,
under a Gideon Bible
are the signs: red letters
exploding on white:
        EXPLOSIVES
In my pocket are
my cigarettes. I clutch
the matches tight.
Hushkapena has become
(for me) (unknown to it)
the place I'll go
if we roll this van
into those final fireworks.

Down the river, around
the bend, riding low
water on its high pitch
comes the silver barge,

an enormous flute
for a latter day Paul Bunyan.
Grabbing our suitcases
and the groceries,
we lurch down the river bank
where the earth is separating
in jagged angles.
We board the board across
flowing water to the first moving barge
crawl around the outer narrow ledge
laced with chicken feed
and make the final leap
onto the silver lady,
*Point Counterpoint
the Second,* just as
the C# moon strikes
a chord across
the sunset clef, and all
      is music, music.

THE BIRDS FOR LUCIE

My sparrow, my lark, my dove, my
mother, I walk down Pelican Street
and all the birds on your walls
begin to sing. You have made
the singing possible, you
have made the birds rise
until, like an Escher, all
the people I know, meet, love,
fit together form to form to
frame, and the wings begin to
move, the body lifts and
aerodynamics take over.

We are flocking South.

A FLOOD WAS RISING

My dear people, let us
love one another, let the rain
breed our words into many
meanings, and the pressure
of our hands. Never before have I
sat on carpet in the middle
of a church and listened
to the rain on the roof,
the rain blurring blue glass
in the long arched windows,
the blurring of the ache

under the ribs, the blurring,
the stained blue glass,
the bluing of the glass and

the staining of the glass ribs,
under the blue glass roof,
under the arched ribs,
My dear people, let us love
one another here on the blue
glass carpet. Lord, give
success to the work of
our hands.

And then he spoke and the word
was not a message from the Lord.
It was a message from himself.
Dear person, it said, let us
love one another. And the rain

THAT'S WHEN NOBODY BELIEVES YOU

The corny old lady ran away from
home to join the circus. And found
it good. And the ducks quacked
goodbye when she left and the people
wanted to touch her, and the seven
year old girl wanted to go to sleep
in her arms, and she found herself
wanting to live instead of wanting
to die by her own hand, and she doesn't
have to hide the implements for suicide
from herself anymore. And when she
is 83 years old and comes tippy-tapping
down the stairs at 2 o'clock in
the morning to hear what the young people
are talking about, is she going to
say: once I had a chance to ride
the Mississippi on a beautiful silver
barge and I turned it down?

FOR 65 THOUSAND DOLLARS

Ms Lily Peter, poet
laureate of Arkansas,
hired the entire Philadelphia
Symphony (complete with
Eugene Ormandy) to come
to Arkansas to perform
the music she commissioned.
This isn't a poem, this is
a fact. And pure poetry.
What Ms Lily does with
cotton, soy beans and
money is
pure poetry.

THE PITTSBURGH TEA PARTY
or
THE NIGHT POINT COUNTERPOINT TURNED HER BACK TO THE SHORE AND PLAYED TO ALL OF US IN THE HOUSEBOATS ON THE RIVER

White beaver on red triangular flag
tops a white staff.
The *Gateway Clipper*'s water wheel
is flashing hot waves behind it.
A yellow box truck crosses
the curved bridge.
The *Debbie B* captures
the flaming sun in her windows.
The multi-colored flags
make a triangle of the *Mark Twain II*.

Tom on English horn and Robin on harp
playing Casterede, turning the clouds,
peak into the Trouble I've Seen.

A silver treble clef
hangs from a silver chain
on the neck of the yellow-suited woman
from Clinton, Iowa, whose son
plays piano like the lapel pin
on her jacket.

9 electric W's
on the other shore
are lighting up
to Handel's Water Music.

The man from Clinton
hands me two pictures
from his Polaroid "They're
not ripe yet." I watch them
bloom.

Like cradles, the boats rock,
we all rock.

The Lady from Clinton mentions Venice
and I am again in a gondola,
wearing blue velvet, trailing
the performing symphony, the opera stars,
down the Grand Canal, drinking
Grand Marnier out of
good blue Venetian glass.
I carefully take each glass
from its cradle of sawdust curls.

The wounded are walking the shore
hunting their bandwagons, wrapping
themselves with their tongues.

Nora Carrington says "Pines of Rome,"
and I am again in the Museum Garden
while the Rome Symphony Orchestra
plays Pines of Rome. The moon is full.
Our men are on it for the second night.

19

Robert is striking up
Down by the Riverside
and I am on a dream carousel
wheeling slower and slower,
One more Time, one more
Time, one more

The sun is setting
in the mouth of the Ohio
filling the O's with light.

The pink river floats the pink boats.
The Navy blue river floats
the Navy blue boats.
The black river turns silver
under the moon, floats
the silver music.

QUALITY OF A TONE

The larger the cavity
within my head, the darker
I play, he said.
The larger the cavity
in my insides, the darker
I work, said I.

WHO HAS THE KEY TO THE HEAD?

Waxed paper hats
fit flush in
the stainless steel
stool.
Gaps like a steel
mouth, snaps
like a steel trap.
At the push of a pedal
dragon flames flash
and the roar of a small
fire dins the steel
base and stops.
No river pollution,
no sweat. The air
smells briefly of
spice fire. Plumb-
ing moves to a
new dimension.

LAKE CHARLES, LOUISIANA

We turn left under
the bridge and come
to the lake, glinting
in the sunlight. Its
riffled surface is
spouting fish. They
ride straight into
the air and flick and tumble
back, even the sound is
silver.

Inside, my spouting
heart rides straight
into the air.

LAKE CHARLES, LOUISIANA II

Afterward she told me
when I said crab,
she thought I said
crap, but knew that
couldn't be one
of my words. She was wrong.
Crap is a word I use
whenever I need it.
It's *vessel* I can't stand
and *moist*, and I
always red-pencil
guilt even though
I can't seem to delete it
any other way.

SLEEPING IN THE MUSEUM

I had better buy the quilt.
Guilt is stitched into its
Lincoln logs (look for the velvet
one.) I rock with the waves.
Lucretia stood in the middle
of this floor and forgot to
open her arms. Sleeping comes
hard when the weight is this
heavy. But the colors are
drenching me, red, ruby, cerise,
pink, purple and orange. I
will try to learn to live without.
(In Lake Charles, they come aboard
with their wallets open, looking
swiftly from one art object to -)
I slowly move to the charted list:
beside Quilt - Blue Mountain design,
I write Sold. It will take my whole
pay. I might as well have the pillow
as well. I have just bought the quilt.
My drought is over.

ALGIERS/NEW ORLEANS

I jump onto the dock
to free the line.

The ferry is free and
telephone calls are a nickel.

Here the houses
are made from barge
planks floated
down river, their
peaked roofs decorated
with wooden lace.

The papier mache pelican
sits on his second story
balcony and flirts
with everyone on
Pelican Street.

Dance, she said and
clapped her hands.

I'm a spy, he said,
leaning through
the wooden bead portieres.
We're going to record
your eating.

I was hungry enough
to eat the Pelican.

Alone in my room
I expected a knock
on the door,
but nobody
knew I was there.

PLANE TO ST LOUIS

Shall I wake the girl
beside me to say:
We're just about to fly over
the tallest monument
in the world?

She rouses, grabs
the paper bag
and is sick all over
the tallest monument
in the world.

ST LOUIS TO NEW ATHENS

By car we drive to New Athens,
distinguished by a hard A beginning,
on the banks of the Kaskaskia River,
the third longest in Illinois, where
the pioneers fought the Kaskaskia Indians
and moved the West, westward.

Point Counterpoint II is nowhere in sight.
Judy Bryan drives me to her home,
and seven-year-old Angela loans me
her room. It is lined with animal
posters whose eyes stare at me
all night. But first:

we go back to the waterfront
where the townspeople are gathered
on a high grassy ridge. Word is:
our boat is on the way.

The musicians are already here,
they have arrived in their vans,
red and blue and green and white
and yellow. After flipping a few
frisbees, they gather in their
chamber groups and by the light
of the parked vans begin to play,
first one group and then another,
while the sun sinks behind the trees.

Up river we can see the bridge
with the turn of road where,
last week, a driver missed the turn
and his body carried down stream
in a channel so deep the divers kept
being swept away while they searched
and searched. "It happens all the time."

The night is cold,
we are wrapped in quilts,
sprayed with OFF.

The police announcement squeals:
POINT COUNTERPOINT IS COMING!

Down river, lights rake the horizon
and the Orchestra Boat sails
into sight, all flags flying!
The crowd surges toward the water
cheering!

Over come the lines, the sound
equipment, I see Paul leveling
the speakers, Jamee hawking
programs, Kathleen settling
the children into proper seats.
The musicians pour on board.
The trumpets take to air, and
the cantilevered roof rises as
the music rises. . . as my spirit
rises.

Angela clutches the quilt close
around us and gasps "Oh Gramma, I mean
Ann," and I am holding Angela tight,
and Robert's voice comes over
the loud speaker, and the first act
(for me, this year) has begun. Here
we go again!

Late and cold and bug-ridden we are, but
the music raises us to the glad-we-came.
Lubos Fiser's *Report* galvanizes us.
The late of the night is forgotten,
swept with music as we are
on that river bank, the Kaskaskia
of Illinois.

Now Marcus is trying to talk the top-dog
into letting the fireworks come
from *this* side of the river. He loses,
consents to be taken to the other shore,
settles his head into the "let's do it"
I know so well, is hustled off to board
the row-boat which will take him
to the firing spot.

We follow the fireworks onto the boat,
I linger back a little to gaze at its
silver sides, move across the gang plank
lay my hand on Robert's. He does a
double-take and says with a grin:
our poet has arrived.

2

For the first time I see
what was hidden to me before:
the whole under-deck of the barge
has been cleared, architectured,
there is SPACE, the new living quarters,
(no more sleeping in the museum)
elegant, carpeted, low-lighted,
with Henry, the full-sized leather seal
resting on a couch. There are
Josh, and Tanya, and Jonathan,
half-remembering me, there are
Jack and Paul and Marilyn,
the old crew and the new,
Dianne from last summer,
Jamee jumping up and down,
Robert and Kathleen, as if
I am coming home to a family
I have known and been separated
from, and now reunion.
In New Athens, Illinois,
Population 2000, on the Kaskaskia
River where I have never been before,
I have in some strange way,
come home.

     Later, later, when Eleanor Scoffield says,
     meeting Marcus in the doorway,
     "Toot-toot, Peanut butter!"
     I see again myself on a post
     at the Iowa State Fair, singing,

because Papa put me there
and told me to: "I went to the animal fair,
all the birds and the beasts were there,"
and the crowd gathered round to hear
and the applause was what I wanted to hear.
So I slept in Angela's room
where the koala bear stared in my eyes all night.
And Angela crept close to every move I made,
and was me at seven.

Is it the carnival? the circus?
the floating show-boat? what urge
to go with the traveling music?
Every time I hear the horns begin
Fanfare to the Common Man
and the roof is rising in the air
against the background of flags,
my insides leap and begin
a rising too that goes straight up
as high as
the fireworks.

INTERMEZZO BY THOMAS STACY

Guest soloist
Principal English horn with
the New York Philharmonic

High E flat
        lingers
    on the air

when I was a little boy
in Arkansas
        lingers
            in the air
On Sunday afternoon
        on the air

listening to the Philharmonic
    on the air   on the radio

        I thought
THAT'S
        where I want to be - want to

High E flat stays   the note stays   in the air

            lingers

I want to be - want to

        le cor anglais

the note stays

I want to stay

    in the air

        lingers   on the air

        (The English horn
        is neither English nor
        a horn.)

STEEL VALLEY

"Do they write
Epics anymore?"
he asked, and here
it is: a long,
low, gray, steel
storage building,
Bessemer, J & L's,
U S Steel, Homestead,
EPIC STEEL.

"This place used to
be festered with
small steel mills,
then U S Steel
came in - " his
circled arms showed
the chronology,
Steel Valley steeling
the people against
Epic poems.

LOCKS AND DAMN #2

This water elevator
sinks us through zo-
ological time,
layers of
earth crust mosaicked
by shell and shark teeth,
stippled with
tiger bones, through coal
down to primordial
morass, to float
us farther. ARMY
US CORPS OF ENGIN-
EERS 1953 down
the Monongahela
(out of the Yough-
iogheny). The
yellow painted edge
of the lock stretches
the sun a thousand
seven hundred
and forty feet.
No Smoking or Open
Flame during Lockage
I dampen my fire.

From a vertical crack
in the lock wall, five
green leaves in their prime

make a live green hand
blessing our descent,
promising in some
inscrutable way
a constant
singing,
a continual
new greening.

CLOUDBURST AT McKEESPORT

Jacomis promised us
water, but he didn't
tell us how. We didn't dream
what contacts he had until
3 raindrops turned into
3 million raindrops and we flattened
our folding chairs and held them
over our heads while the whole
Symphony doing "Concerto
for Percussion" played
the best storm music
any of us had ever heard
and the fireworks wetting down
across the Youghiogheny
were no match (even dry) for
the LIGHTning which knew
what fireWORKS were all about.

AFTER THE SHERIFF CAME
IN THE MIDDLE OF THE NIGHT

When the rain began
on the metal roof,
I thought
it was the sheriff's men
spraying us with gasoline
to set us on fire.

When the waves whipped us
against the moving dock,
I thought
the sheriff's men
were trying to chop
the boat in two.

When the sheriff came aboard
with his men
in the middle of the night
asking for "Mr Boodroo"
we told him
if he jailed anybody,
he'd have to jail us all.

HERB, GROCERY POET, LEAVES THE BOAT

There you are at the end of a mile-long grocery aisle!
I am waving goodbye with a mouldy stalk of celery.
You wave back with an O Cedar mop.
Each time I try to run toward you, the floor is covered
with Cheerios that slipped off the shelf.
Or a can of kidney beans hits the floor and explodes.
I do a long slide on Lux Flakes.

The aisle gets longer, you are receding.
Cheerio, I shout. Your shout back is lost amongst
the yellow brick cheese. You yell, I *think* you yell:
PRODuce! PRODuce! or is it ProDUCE! ProDUCE?

THEY DIDN'T WANT US DOCKED
AT THEIR FISHING PIER

Dear Herb, An hour
after you left, all
hell broke loose and
Robert cut the telephone
lines and was headed
back to Pittsburgh
and the talking broke
down, the person to
person approach, and
fifty feet on the River
was enough to break
the Allegheny's back.
      I need, said
the publisher, to keep
the peace between
the fine arts committee
and the fishing sports
so there will be
money for next year.
Next year, says Robert,
I won't be back, next
year or ever, and
the publisher's hopes
for raising the cultural
level in that town
(how he had dreamed
his plan at the Sunday
night wine and cheese
affair) fell to a new
low like the water level
in the Allegheny.
                    cheers,

UNDERWATER SENSES

I hear the bell buoy moan.

I do not see the barracuda
move from left to right.

What is a fishy smell
to a fish?

Why do I always feel
as if an anchor pulls me down?

Why do I taste salt
even in fresh water?

CANNED HEAT

I do understand partly about
your wanting your poetry cooked
to a certain heat (or else it gives
no warmth) and if you can't warm your
hands by it, what good is temperature.
Inversions are troubling cities
all over the nation, and I have been
standing here on my head for
several years now and nobody pays
the slightest attention. Outrageous
lines have become our stock in
trade, and nothing I might say
would surprise you, but do
beware of the rusted poem,
the one whose side is
bulging.

ARTIST

So there stands
this moment in time
with his teeth marks
on it.

George, the architect,
came into the galley,
saw the doughnut platter
beside the coffee pot.

Someone had taken a bite
out of a doughnut,
put it back on the plate.

Carefully, deliberately,
George took one bite
out of every doughnut.

CLASSES OVER IN ANOTHER RIVER TOWN

Goodbye Philip, I want
to fill your dimples with
my thumbs. Curly-haired
Joe Fall, I couldn't tell you
that another Joey Fall
proposed to me before anyone
else did, on a long ago night
when the world and Joey were mine.
Gentle, quietly determined Keith
telling me maybe I shouldn't
wear the left-over price tags
dangling from my ears, 'a distraction
perhaps for a serious conferring.'
Nymph-like Margie glowing
from success, tearing up at leaving
before the end. Volital Gordon
seductive in his choker and his
white clinging suit open to
his ribs, wanting to steal
my lines, saying I should
give them to him. And Porter
saying he didn't know his tongue
cut me off at the knees, over & over
& over again, playing leader in
follow the leader.
Pixie Ginnie with her small case
is coming into her sure and artful
self. And Rachel, like my daughter
in critical mood, disapproving,
"You have to be calm" as if she
needed serenity, not wanting me
as I am. The mother she tangled with,
my daughter who tangled with me.

What did they learn from me?
Anything about poetry?

SINKING: MAD HANNAH IV

I do not know at what point I decided
to sink or swim. I pushed the shore away,
struck out for Hannibal.
      Water has never been
anything to buoy me up. But I have let
the heat of soapy water move over
my arms, hold my elbows, encase
my shoulder blades.
      Now Mad Hannah walks
the old canal carrying conversations
in her carpet bag. Now and then
she settles on a stone and takes one out
and wonders if she ever spoke these words
out loud to anyone.

DEAR MAESTRO

I came to Greenville to
audition for your
orchestra.
Willie Washington
drove me all over
the Waterfront
looking for
your boat. Waterways
had never heard of
Point Counterpoint the Second.

I couldn't tell whether
you had come and gone or
whether you were someplace
downstream bucking water.
The filled-up-hotel manager
said he'd take me in or
take me home and cancelled
somebody's reservation.

I'm sorry you missed the
boat. I am working my way
East playing trombone.

DREAM TRAIN WITH CIRCUS

The golden train glides trackless
filled with lolling figures
in curious clothes, whose friends
are these who move through my sleeplessness
draped in each other's arms.
Their fantasy is not mine
but they are not strangers.
I know them all, or want to.
The hysteria here in their
garments, raucous color that
comforts me, comes to my need
in clown costumes, faces serene
under paint, even with red bulb
noses, triangular eyes. Their
survival is mine, they share
their rest with me. Awake I
have dreamed them up.
The golden train glides through me
and I take them in.

OR DREAMING

How clearly I remember things
that didn't happen. The night
my mother danced in that black
leotard and was grace itself,
she had been dead for twenty
years and I was not drunk
or dreaming.

FOUR HOURS ON/FOUR HOURS OFF

I was on the River Chart job,
my flashlight casting an eerie
shaft through its blue plastic cover.
Paul Tracey was on binoculars
to spot the buoys marking the channel.
In his South African accent he kept
saying, "That's a pointy one,
must be red on the starboard."
We should have caught on sooner
that he was color Blind!

Southbound traffic on the Mississippi
has the right of way, so when we saw
a ship coming, or heard it on the radio,
(Kindly Marianne approaching Lock 27)
we would call ahead and see whether
the captain of the Marianne wanted
a one whistle or a two whistle pass,
Portside to portside being one,
starboard to starboard, two. Radio
channel 16 was always open so we
could hear who was coming and going.

The night was clear.
We were zooming along catching
all the proper markers. Paul (folk
singer) Tracey choreographed the whistle
blow when he was asked to perform
with his long prehensile thumb
which can reach over and play the second
string of the guitar neck!

And that whistle is a
pure dominant chord
that rings out over the river
like a message from a pipe organ.

The Myra Eckstein was stuck up-river
on a sand-bar, farther down the Logan
was in the same predicament,
the channel was narrow, when at 11 o'clock,
(10 pilot house time - ship's clock)
the Captain went to eat and take a rest.
Marcus took over the throttles, Lorenzo
was on the radar, I on charts, Paul
on binoculars/buoys and North we went!

The night was clear and balmy.
Camaraderie in the pilot house
was mellow. Coffee cups were filled
often enough. Someone of the 16
people on board wandered in and out,
laughter, checking back and forth,
only the slightest trickle of apprehension,
only a slight tautness of muscle,
everyone checking, doing his job,
moving steadily through the night,
between the islands, trying to make
everything come through the night vision
that changes everything. Distances waver,
the looming black shadows against black
loom larger and closer, the straight channel
begins to bend, and we move through the night
all 195 feet of boat, with a 38 foot beam,
no rudder.

We are traveling (Come in Point Counterpoint
Two. *What* are you?) Point Counterpoint II
to the Accusable. We are a self-propelled barge
195 feet long. 38 feet wide. With the American
Wind Symphony Orchestra. Out of Pittsburgh.
Headed for Keokuk. Crew and family aboard. (I
am second cook. Right now I am chart reader.)
and the channel, curving to portside looks
mighty narrow for a barge, a 9 barge tow,
heading South with the current to pass us on
either the one whistle or two whistle side.
We are 38 feet wide and rudderless.
Three engines control our speed ahead or back.
The left tachometer is not working.
It went out during the flooding in the Ohio.
But that was last week.
This is tonight.

"Come on through the narrows," says the Captain
on the 9 barge tow. "I don't want to meet you there."
Roger. Roger and Out.   We don't want to meet him
either. We haven't told him we are making 6 knots
an hour at best. We should have told him.

We plow ahead through the water,
the muddy rolling waves turn into ploughed
red-brown earth, furrows of red-brown earth,
as if any one of them could stop us hard.
We know it is red-brown water, but the illusion
of solid earth is complete.

Suddenly it is as if we have come over the edge
of the world and the whole sky ahead of us

is alight with moving light from horizon to horizon.
We are falling forward over the edge of the earth.
No, they are falling on us. All the light
of heaven and earth is falling on us. QUICK! How
do we escape! Hold on, says Marcus,
Here we go. We brace ourselves for what we know
is about to happen. There is no place else
to go. A sudden Crunching sound of sand
under propellors, we are beginning to swing,
we are whirling, through the dark the riverbank
is moving so fast I cannot keep track of
the numbered signs, I *must* keep track of
the numbered signs, only if I keep track can we
come back to our direction, can we start again
on some reasonable route when this nightmare
of whirling is over, which it must be, must be
soon, but we mustn't hit hard at any point,
we are unique, there is no boat under the sun
or the night sky like us, no one to replace
us if we sink in the middle of the Mississippi
River.

But we are as vulnerable as all those river boats,
we are *more* vulnerable than all those river boats,
and we have been given the right-of-way by
a generous river captain who then changed
his mind (he didn't know how SLOW we were!) and
his fleet of barges was charging down on us
like a lighted city - bigger than all New Athens,
it looked like all New York - and we did the only thing
we could do. Marcus and Paul and Lorenzo and I,
we ran her aground. To save the boat, to save

ourselves, we crashed her into the safest place
we could think of - a sand bar island that
would either be our friend or sink us and
we would soon find out which.

I shall leave out the scene of
the Captain arriving in the pilot house.
He had a right to be mad, of course.
Off course was what we were, but with
our best judgement, we amateurs had
performed the best music we knew how
on throttles, binoculars, radar and charts,
we just had to play it in a minor key, that's all.

Hours later, almost dawn, we had backed
and forthed enough (praying there was
no hole in the boat) (there wasn't) to
take to the river again. Jubilant
at survival, muted by mistakes. The cross
tension was almost enough to drive the engines.
And we sailed into Keokuk
on the Coast of Iowa
where they welcomed us
as if we were their own.

BLOODLINES

I am always in trouble
when someone speaks in banshee
and without thinking, I reply.

Meet me, meet me, anywhere
you like (not over water)
and I will come as far as
the edge of my map.

FRIENDS

So when my friend said
"My kite string is
covered with seaweed,"
what could I do? I said,
"So's mine."

ROBERT BOUDREAU, MAN OF THE YEAR

"It may just be that there is no greater
innovative force in American music
than Robert Boudreau." *Time*

So there was that year, twenty-some years ago,
when he came out of Juilliard
with his horn, and jobs were scarce,
so he climbed on his dream and tried
to make it fly. Went down
a Pittsburgh street and turned in
at the Heinz pickle factory.

The rest is history.
Concerto for pickles came out of it,
boats and orchestras and commissioned
music came out of it, cleaned-up
river fronts came out of it, and
people touched by music from Maine
to Texas.

The first time I saw Pittsburgh,
(I'd hitched a ride from Iowa City to
the Sea) I could hardly see Pittsburgh,
drowned as she was in that dark daytime
cloud. The last time I flew over Pittsburgh
I could see that Golden Triangle
of rivers, where the Allegheny and
Monongahela come together to make
the Ohio, and that Golden Triangle
was as clear as a gift down below.

That year they gave Robert a medal.
And this year? There is the Swedish
Consul General making Robert, by
order of the King of Sweden, Knight
First Class, Royal Order of the North
Star! Where does he go from here!

Back to Mars. Pennsylvania, that is,
back to the goat farm he runs
in the winters. He is, after all,
as he says, "just a chicken farmer
from Massachusetts."

MOVING OUT

It is time to move on.
Let me move quietly,
moaning is obsolete.
The wailing wall
has been torn down
and the boards used
for plank walking.
Hold the door while
I try for a long last
smile. Hold the door
for all these suitcases.
Hold the door. Hold
me.

HOME ON THE MVA

So I am on the Mississippi Valley Airplane,
elbows pressed to my sides to make myself as
small as possible, no other way to get 14
of us in these small seats, one on each
side of this narrow aisle, and the engines
are started, and we begin to taxi -
- *in a circle*? *what is this*? yes, we
are coming back to the gateway, and out
comes, not a new passenger, no room in
this packed sardine-can of a plane,
but the take-off checker, who rushes out
to the rear of the plane and takes from
its hook the tail brace which he had placed
there to support the plane while the bags
and passengers were loaded. He waves us
on. Now we are free to leave.
                                        We taxi
to the end of the runway, we are the only
plane moving on this prairie field.
We struggle into the air and dip a wing
at the low slung shelter and head
into the strange cloud formation
hanging over the river. We are too
far from town to find the waterfront,
Point Counterpoint is somewhere there
under that dull sky, gleaming her own
silver self. The adventure is over.

But wait. What is that passenger
pulling from his briefcase? What is

that colorful catalogue that fills
the space between him and the seat
ahead of him? It is, how could it be,
it *is* a catalogue of FIREWORKS,
pictures exploding in brilliant rays
of color, in gleaming streaks of light!

Order No. 1098 for the Presidential
Prestigious Pylons, the Flaming
Princess in shades of red and orange,
the Captured Cantata, a Veritable
Fountain of Multicolored Star Heads,
lifting your Spirits as it Lifts your
Eyes! And yes, Handel's Music for
the Royal Fireworks is running through
my head and down there under that
soft grey haze, the Musical Queen
Herself - Point Counterpoint the Second
is being the Royal Visitor from
some outer Space, one man's Dream,
as it were, and above the flying flags,
the EXPLOSIVES B are striking the air
in wondrous Color, the Royal Fireworks,
Handel and all, have Begun!

THE LAST TIME

The last time I saw Paul Tracey
was on New Year's Eve
on the Johnny Carson Show
when he sang one of his wild
South African folksongs
to his own swift guitar.

The last time I saw Elsie Neal
was on the Mr Rogers TV show
where she as Miss Elsie, the Craft
Lady, brought Mr Rogers
a toy airplane made of
empty spools and rubber bands.

The last time I saw Frank Ross,
master potter, he was barrelling
along in his little panel truck
waving out the window
at our little airplane
(spools and rubber bands?)
barrelling along, trying
to climb high enough
to make a straight shot for
Chicago.

FOR FRANK ROSS, MASTER POTTER, 19? - 1980

You, yes, you in my mirror
made by you and traded to me
for copies of my books -
couldn't you have been more careful?
Driving to the boat, you let
a truck bash you broadside
and splatter the tears from
the Mississippi to the Eastern Shore.

These bowls of yours I bought for gifts
(from the museum, before we ever met)
for friends back home, and found
I couldn't bear to give them away.
The careful firing, the grouting,
the colors of earth you loved,
one clear blue line for sky.

"You have to make 12 mugs
a week for roof and food,"
you told your kids.
Basics: your art was based
on basics, and your own keen eye,
the deftness of your hands.

When I look in your/my mirror
I do not see me. I see
your human face, warm-eyed,
bearded, your giving self.
Through water, I see you.

STORM ON THE MISSISSIPPI

Here on this snowing day, I put my feet
toward my fireplace fire, and suddenly
my soles are burning and I am running
barefoot across the burning hot metal
of the top of the boat, Point Counterpoint II,
running to pull the flags and furl them
against the storm, the wind is rising,
I am running running in place as I pull
the flag staffs out of their position holes,
running so I will not scorch the bottoms
of my bare feet, the storm is pitching
the waves on the river behind us where we
have just left the safe port of Quincy, Illinois,
where they couldn't raise enough money
to invite us to stay, for the orchestra
to perform, for the artists to perform,
but this storm is performing and I am
dancing on the top of the boat as we
pull up the Mississippi and the sky has
turned green and the light is making
the trees purple along the shore and
the backdrop for this performance is
long shadowed and abstract color
and form and all of the flags are
flapping crazily and the choreography
is coming as fast as I am moving and
I am trying to save the flags and save
my feet and save myself from being

lashed by the wind over the side of
the ship into the lashed water which is
rising higher and higher in angry waves
and the rain is beginning and the curtains
of water are flashing down almost
horizontally and I am moving so fast
I can't see my hands stop
and I have finished the final flag,
hand over hand down the ladder, slip-
ping and sliding into the shelter of
the deckhouse - and turn, just in time
to see, flashing past the porthole,
the four-hundred pound speakers, blown
off the top of the deck disappearing
into the solid flesh of the Mississippi
River water, swallowed whole by
the Father of Waters.

LETTER FOR ZIMMER THE TIME HE PLAYED
FAIRY GODFATHER ON HIS TUBA

Dear Paul,   You were right. I was a natural
for it. But whoever thought one could fall
in love with a whole symphony orchestra and
a boat. My world was turning dark, but on
the Mississippi River my grief jumped
overboard. Or was it the Achafalya?

Now I know what I want on my tombstone:

> Late in life she
> ran away from home and
> joined the circus.

TIME ZONES ON THE RIVERS

It is nine fifteen on the Mississippi,
ten fifteen here on the Shenandoah.
The moon, one night past full, rolls
in its own course. The Mississippi
loops to the sea. The Shenandoah
flows North. We are riding our course.
I have cursed rivers and found
my home on one of them. If I
force the current, I cannot come
back to the Mississippi, one border
of my life. I dream of water.
The backs of my hands are rivers
and deltas. I trace the bayous,
late, late, I follow the current
and the river flows. I shall try
to stop drinking and let
the river flow.

Dear poet of Arkansas,
I love your frogs.
They come to me from our pond,
on this meadow above
the Shenandoah. Your
Mississippi has been home to you
but I came to water late,
having almost drowned
in the Raccoon which flows into
your river. The water moving.
I was always moving, thinking

I was hunting an island, not
knowing I was hunting
the water, the current.
It takes a long time to live
said Jim Wright who knew
the Ohio. It takes a long
time to know where home is.
Transient on the Potomac,
on the Snake, on the Red,
the Raccoon, I clung
to the bank, but finally
I am learning
to ride the river,
to float alone,
to ride the current North.
It is 11:15 here on the Charles.

POETRY FROM ALICE JAMES BOOKS